W9-BZC-474

Also by Steve Goodier

One Minute Can Change a Life
Riches of the Heart
Joy Along the Way
Prescription for Peace

Please see the Quick Order Form at the
back of this book.

Touching Moments

60-second readings that touch the mind and the heart

Steve Goodier

First Edition

Life Support System ♥ Publishing, Inc.
P.O. Box 237 Divide, CO 80814
www.LifeSupportSystem.com

Touching Moments

60-second readings that touch the mind and the heart

By Steve Goodier

Life Support System♡Publishing, Inc.
P.O. Box 237 Divide, CO 80814

Library of Congress Card Number: 2001116662

ISBN 1-929664-04-4 (Soft cover)

Cover design: Brent Stewart & Darrel Voth

Contents

Living With Romance

One woman tells this story about her parents. She says that they had not been out together in quite some time. One Saturday, as her mother was finishing the dinner dishes, her father stepped up behind her.

"Would you like to go out, girl?" he asked.

Not even turning around, her mother quickly replied, "Oh, yes, I'd love to!"

They had a wonderful evening, and it wasn't until the end of it that her dad confessed. His question had actually been directed to the family dog, lying near her mom's feet on the kitchen floor.

When should romance flicker and die from a caring relationship? When a couple decides to marry? Or after children are born? Or during the mature years?

I love the attitude of one woman who believed her life should never be without romance. She found herself seated at a banquet next to a gen-

1

tleman in his eighties – about her age. She stared at him until she had his attention.

Finally, she said, "Please forgive me for staring at you like this, but I can't help it. You see, you look exactly like my third husband!"

"Oh," he responded. "How many times have you been married?"

With a warm smile and a twinkle in her eye, she patted his hand and answered, "Twice!"

Many find love, but some will also find romance – and keep it.

Heart to Heart

In the 1960s, a National Aeronautics and Space Administration team working on the Apollo moon mission took some astronauts to Arizona, where the terrain of the Navajo Reservation looks very much like the lunar surface. With all the trucks and large vehicles were two figures that were dressed in full lunar spacesuits.

NASA official Charles Phillip Whitedog tells that a Navajo sheep rancher and his son were watching the strange creatures walking about. The father did not speak English and his son asked for him what the strange creatures were. It was explained to that they were astronauts training to go to the moon. The man became excited and asked if he could send a message to the moon with the crew.

NASA personnel grabbed a tape recorder and the old Navajo spoke into it. When asked to translate, his son refused. The NASA people played the recording for other natives on the reservation, each of whom smiled or chuckled and likewise re-

3

fused to translate. Finally, they paid someone to translate the rancher's message:

"Watch out for these guys, they come to take your land."

World history is replete with examples of people "watching out" for one another. But I believe today's world is learning the higher value of keeping faith. One writer accurately says, "On the day when we can fully trust each other, there will be peace on earth."

Keeping faith is essential between nations and within nations. It keeps the peace. Keeping faith is essential between companies and their customers. It creates good will. And keeping faith is essential between friends and within families. It builds bonds of love that no amount of adversity can break. Invincible bonds are forged upon the anvil of trust.

If people like you, they'll give you a hand. But if they trust you, they'll give you their heart. And heart to heart, we can face anything together.

P.S.

"Experience is what you get when you don't get what you want."

When You Judge Yourself

Charles Allen, in his book *Victories in the Valleys of Life* (Fleming H. Revell, 1981), tells the story of a man who, one wintry day, went to traffic court in Wichita, Kansas, not knowing court had been canceled because of a blizzard. A few days later he wrote this letter:

"I was scheduled to be in court February 23rd, at 12:15 p.m., concerning a traffic ticket. Well, I was there as scheduled and, to my surprise, I was the only one there. No one had called to tell me that the court would be closed, so I decided to go ahead with the hearing as scheduled, which meant that I had to be the accuser, the accused and the judge. The citation was for going 46 miles per hour in a 35-mile-per-hour zone. I had the speed alert on in my car, set for 44 miles per hour; and as the accuser, I felt that I was going over 35 miles per hour, but as the accused, I know that I was not going 46 miles per hour. As judge, and being the understand-

6

ing man that I am, I decided to throw it out of court this time. But it had better not happen again."

He had a rare opportunity to judge himself and took full advantage. On the other hand, we probably judge ourselves all day long. We may even react more harshly to our own mistakes and errors than we would ever react to those same shortcomings in others.

Two thousand years ago a Roman writer named Publilius Syrus observed, "How unhappy are they who cannot forgive themselves." Whether dealing with others or with ourselves, it usually helps to err on the side of grace. Do you need to be gentler with yourself?

Three Important Things

You've heard it said, "Be nice to your kids. They'll choose your nursing home." Well, there may be other and more important reasons for being careful how we treat one another.

I think that U.S. industrialist Charles M. Schwab may have gotten it right. At age 72, Schwab was sued for a large sum of money. Many high-profile persons would have settled out of court, but Schwab went through with it and eventually won the suit.

Before he left the witness stand, he asked permission of the court to make a statement of a personal nature.

This is what he said: "I am an old man, and I want to say that ninety percent of my troubles have been due to my being good to other people. If you younger folk want to avoid trouble, be hard-boiled and say no to everybody. You will then walk through life unmolested, but..." and here a broad

8

smile lit up his face, "you will have to do without friends, and you won't have much fun."

Maybe that's why Henry James said, "Three things in human life are important: The first is to be kind. The second is to be kind. And the third is to be kind." It's a vital part of a whole and happy life.

P.S.

"If you're looking to find the key to the Universe, I have some bad news and some good news. The bad news is: there is no key to the Universe. The good news is: it has been left unlocked." ~ Unknown

What Do You Know?

Did you hear about the man who attempted skydiving for the first time? His parachute didn't open. Then his auxiliary chute failed. Now he found himself in free fall with no more options.

Then a strange thing happened. He spotted something coming up towards him from the ground at a high rate of speed. It was a man! When he was sure they would pass one another without a collision, he shouted down to the figure, "Do you know anything about parachutes?"

"No!" the man called back. "Do you know anything about gas stoves?"

A little bit of technological knowledge could have been helpful in both cases. But it has never just been about how much we *know*.

I read that the world's body of knowledge doubled from 1900 to 1950. In other words, knowledge that took thousands of years to accumulate doubled in only fifty years. It then doubled again between 1950 and 1965. In just fifteen years. It is

11

estimated that the world's body of knowledge doubled once more between 1965 and 1970 and now doubles every five years. Amazing! We can never keep up with all there is to learn.

But perhaps more important than how much any of us *knows* is how consistently we *act* on the knowledge we have. We certainly need enough knowledge to live fruitful and constructive lives, but even knowledge will not serve well if we neglect to use it.

You may know that material things don't bring lasting happiness. Will you actively pursue things of the heart and spirit?

You may know peace comes when you forgive. Will you decide to put down that grudge and leave it behind?

You may know that any decision made from fear alone is likely to be wrong. Will you choose the path of courage, even if that path seems hard to navigate?

Most of us know important principles about effective living. But in the end, what we know to be true is of no consequence – the decisions we make are everything. And if we apply well even the little we know, we can be healthy, happy and hopeful.

A Laugh A Day

"She who laughs, lasts." At least that was Theresa of Avila's philosophy. Theresa, a Spanish nun who founded the reformed order of the Carmelites in 1562, used to look for novices who knew how to laugh, eat and sleep. She believed that if they ate heartily, they were healthy; if they slept well, they were more than likely free of serious sin; and if they laughed, they had the necessary disposition to survive a difficult life.

Abraham Lincoln must have also known that laughter is good medicine. In writing about Lincoln's Civil War years, author Richard Hanser says that on September 22, 1862, the War Cabinet was summoned to the White House for a special session. Lincoln was reading a book as everyone came in. Secretary of War Stanton later said this of the meeting: "Finally the president turned to us and said, 'Gentlemen, did you ever read anything of Artimus Ward? Let me read a chapter that is very funny.'"

13

The president then read aloud a skit called "Highhanded Outrage at Utica." Stanton was furious, but Lincoln read on and, at the end, he laughed heartily. "Gentlemen," he asked, "why do you not laugh? With the fearful strain that is upon me day and night, if I did not laugh, I should die. And you need this medicine as much as I do." It was at this same session that the president pulled a paper from his tall hat and read aloud the now immortalized Emancipation Proclamation.

He's right – we may likely die without frequent and sustained doses of laughter. After all, they who laugh, last.

Have you had your belly laugh today?

Getting The Best From Those You Lead

A teacher was sitting at her desk grading papers when her first grade class came back from lunch. One of her students informed her, "Robert has to go to the principal's office."

"I wonder why?" the teacher mused.

"Because he's a following person," the child replied.

"A what?" the teacher asked.

"It came over the loudspeaker: 'The following persons are to go to the office.'"

Some people are "leading people" and some are "following people." And actually, we are each followers and leaders at various times. But if you are ever in a leadership position, this advice from college football coaching legend "Bear" Bryant about how to get the best from those you're leading can be useful.

"I'm just a plow hand in Arkansas," Bear said, "but I have learned how to hold a team to-

15

gether. How to lift some men up, how to calm down others, until finally they've got one heartbeat together, a team. There are just three things I'd ever say: 'If anything goes bad, I did it. If anything goes semi-good, then we did it. If anything goes real good, then you did it.' That's all it takes to get people to win football games for you."

I suspect that's all it takes to get people to be effective in any situation. For leaders are only as good as those who follow them, and followers are at their best when leaders are quick to give credit for successes.

British classical scholar Benjamin Jowett put it like this: "The way to get things done is not to mind who gets the credit for doing them." That's especially good to know when you're a "leading person."

P.S.

"We hope that when the insects take over the world, they will remember with gratitude how we took them along on all our picnics.
~ Bill Vaughan

If You Had It To Do Over

One woman announced, "I intend to live forever! So far so good...." But the length of our lives is not the real issue; it's the quality and meaning that matter. Not the years in a life, but the life in the years.

When asked what he wanted to be remembered for when his life was over, Leo Buscaglia replied, "I want to be remembered as somebody who lived life fully and with passion. I've been asked to write my epitaph and I have always thought that the perfect one for my tombstone would be, 'Here lies Leo who died living.'"

I want to die living. And I want to be remembered as one who lived with purpose, joy and verve. I want to spend my time learning what goes into a whole and happy life, then building that life the best I can.

Sociologist Tony Campolo told about a study in which fifty people over the age of 90 were asked to reflect upon their lives. "If you had it to do

18

over again," they were asked, "what would you do differently?" Though there were many answers, three responses dominated. Here they are:

First, many respondents answered, "I would reflect more." Do you ever feel that too much time is spent in "doing" and not enough spent thinking about *what* you are doing and *why* you are doing it?

Second, they said, "I would risk more." Do you think that important opportunities either have been or might be forfeited because of your fear to take a necessary risk?

Finally, they said, "I would do more things that would live on after I died." Do you feel that you are immersed in something bigger and more enduring than your own existence?

Reflect more. Risk more. Leave a legacy. These are what our elders say they would do the second time around.

But why wait for a second time around? Every new day is a second chance! Reflect more today – it will reveal to you what is truly important. Risk more today – take a chance on making that dream come alive. Get involved with something which makes a difference in this world – and a beautiful legacy is what you will leave behind.

Like Leo Buscaglia, I want to live fully and with passion. And if all my plans don't work out as I had hoped, I'm still betting that I will have more fun!

Let It Shine!

While attending a conference, I returned to my motel room late one evening. The overhead light outside my door was burned out and I had difficulty finding the keyhole. When I managed to open the door, I felt around the wall for a light switch. I found a plate where a switch was once installed...but no switch.

Not discouraged easily, I remembered spotting a lamp by the bed when I deposited my luggage earlier in the day. I found the bed in the dark and felt around until I found the lamp, but when I switched it on, nothing happened! Now what?

Though I knew that it was dark outside my window since the outdoor light was broken, I thought that perhaps if I opened the curtains I might be able to use the light from the street to find another lamp. So I made my way slowly across the room to the drapes and...no drawstring! (Have you ever had days like that?)

20

I finally stumbled around until I found a desk lamp that actually worked! That evening I discovered in a whole new way just how dark the world can be and how necessary light is.

But even more necessary than physical light is the light that shines from people – that light which illumines these dark recesses of the spirit and warms the heart. The light of love and compassion and faith. Because, for many people, the world is a dark and lonely place.

Last December I received a letter from Robin in Mexico City who said this about the darkness around her: "Yesterday I bought a Christmas decoration. It's a plastic star, maybe 18 inches across, strung with small white and gold Christmas lights. I hung it in my living room window last night. It looks so beautiful from outside – even better than I had hoped! I live on the second floor of a five-story government housing project building. The building where I live is tucked away where few people go. Not a whole lot of folks see my lighted star. As long as I have it plugged in, that star shines bravely and brightly out into the cold night. It shines on regardless of whether anyone is around to see it or not. And I know that anyone who *does* see it must be heartened by it – it's that lovely.

"I got to thinking, 'Isn't that the way *we* should be? Shouldn't our lives in some way shine out into the cold night – regardless of whether or

21

not anyone admires them? It's certainly nice when someone notices us and is encouraged or heartened. But, after all, isn't it the *shining* itself that is most important?'"

It *is* the shining that is important, whether or not you feel as if you are making a difference. For someone today just may be stumbling in discouragement or sadness or fear and in need of some light.

So let your light shine. Whatever light you offer may be a beacon of hope and encouragement in someone's darkness. And if you feel that your light is no more than a candle in a forest, remember this – there isn't enough darkness in all the world to put out the light of one small candle.

Will you let your light shine?

P.S.

"Be who you are and say what you feel, because those who mind don't matter and those who matter don't mind." ~ *Dr. Seuss*

Because We Don't Have Ear-Lids

Patricia Goldman, as vice chairperson of the National Transportation Safety Board, used to tell a story about how poorly airline passengers listen. She says that one flight attendant, who was frustrated by passenger inattentiveness during her what-to-do-in-an-emergency talk, changed the wording. This is what she actually said:

"When the mask drops down in front of you, place it over your naval and continue to breathe normally."

Not a single passenger noticed.

We have eyelids, but we do not have ear-lids. To compensate, we learn to listen selectively – to turn our listening on and off. But if you have ever been listened to, really listened to, you know how powerful that experience is. You can likewise listen more effectively to others by applying these four important listening principles:

24

- Listen with your eyes. Make eye contact with the speaker. Learn to concentrate on the moment at hand and clear your mind of distractions.
- Listen with your ears. It is impossible to listen when you are speaking.
- Listen with your mind. Let go of preconceived ideas about what you *think* the speaker is saying. Keep your mind open, even if you suspect you will dislike what you are about to hear.
- Listen with your heart. Be concerned for and genuinely interested in the person to whom you are listening. That will speak louder than anything you actually say.

Listening with your eyes, your ears, your mind and your heart is not only effective, it will create an almost magical bond between you and others that can be achieved in no other way. Dr. Karl Menninger stated, "Listening is a magnetic and strange thing, a creative force. The friends who listen to us are the ones we move toward. When we are listened to, it creates us, makes us unfold and expand."

We all need a friend who really listens. And we can all be one.

25

The Power Of Together

The poet Rupert Brooke set out to travel by boat from England to America. Everyone on deck had someone there to see him or her off – everyone except him. Rupert Brooke felt lonely, terribly lonely. Watching the hugging and kissing and good-byes, he wished he had someone to miss him.

The poet saw a youngster and asked his name. "William," the boy answered.

"William," he asked, "would you like to earn a few shillings?"

"Sure I would! What do I have to do?"

"Just wave to me as I leave," the lonely man instructed.

It is said that money can't buy love, but for six shillings young William waved to Rupert Brooke as the boat pulled out. The poet writes, "Some people smiled and some cried, some waved white handkerchiefs and some waved straw hats. And I? I had William, who waved at me with his

26

red bandana for six shillings and kept me from feeling completely alone."

We are all lonely at times. But here was a man who was strong enough to admit his loneliness. One psychotherapist says that a necessary first step toward coping with loneliness is for people to feel free simply admitting they are lonely. For once we recognize it, then we can do something about it.

What can we do? Reach out to friends and family. Too many people are lonely because they have been building walls instead of bridges.

We can also find others who may be lonely and help fill their emptiness. The world is full of them. Mother Teresa used to describe loneliness as "the biggest disease" of our time. And the loneliest do not all reside in nursing homes, nor do they all live by themselves.

Finally, we can recognize that, spiritually, we are not alone. This is a time for us to dig deep into our spiritual being.

Lily Tomlin quipped, "We're all in this alone." But, of course, that isn't true. And great joy comes from discovering the power in the word "together."

Spirit Of Love

Henry Drummond has said, "The moments when you have really lived are the moments when you have done things in the spirit of love."

Here is a story (possibly apocryphal, but powerful nevertheless) about a man who acted in the spirit of love and what he consequently learned.

The story comes from Zig Ziglar's book, *See You At The Top* (Pelican Publishing Co., 1982). He tells about an old man who stood on a Virginia riverbank many years ago. He was waiting to cross the river and, since it was bitterly cold and there were no bridges, he would have to "catch a ride" to the other side. After a lengthy wait he spotted a group of horsemen approaching. He let the first one pass, then the second, third, fourth and fifth. One rider remained. As he drew abreast, the old man looked him in the eye and said, "Sir, would you give me a ride across the river?"

The rider immediately replied, "Certainly." Once across the river, the old man slid to the

28

ground. "Sir," the rider said before leaving. "I could not help but notice that you permitted all the other men to pass without asking for a ride. Then, when I drew abreast, you immediately asked me to carry you across. I am curious as to why you didn't ask them and you did ask me."

The old man quietly responded, "I looked into their eyes and could see no love and knew in my own heart it would be useless to ask for a ride. But when I looked into your eyes, I saw compassion, love and the willingness to help. I knew you would be glad to give me a ride across the river.

The rider was touched. "I'm grateful for what you are saying," he said. "I appreciate it very much." With that, Thomas Jefferson turned and rode off to the White House.

Ziglar reminds us that our eyes are the windows of our souls. Then he asks a pointed question: "If you had been the last rider, would the old man have asked you for a ride?"

A good question! For it is said that others will know us by our love. Some will see it in the things we do and some in the things we say. And a few perceptive souls, like the old man, may catch a glimmer of a loving and generous spirit in the expression of kind eyes.

However it shows, may you be known by your love.

Keys We Must Have

A funny story tells about three high school seniors who went to New York for their senior trip. When they arrived in the city, they went immediately to one of the finest hotels and registered for a room. They were assigned a room on the 30th floor.

After settling in, they decided to go see the sights. They toured Manhattan, the Empire State Building, Wall Street and the Statue of Liberty. They finally returned to their hotel utterly exhausted.

When they asked the desk clerk for the key to their room, he said, "I am sorry, the elevators are not running." He told them that they could either wait or use the stairway. The thought of a soft bed was irresistible, so they decided to climb the stairs – all thirty stories.

One of the boys had an idea. "On the way up, each of us will tell the funniest story we know for ten flights of stairs," he suggested. The other two agreed and started to climb. When they reached the tenth floor, they were still going strong. By the twentieth floor, their legs were rubber and they panted for breath. The steps grew harder to climb and the one whose turn it was to tell a funny story said, "I'm sorry, I'm just too tired to talk."

They trudged on in silence. When they reached the 29th floor, one of them began to laugh. He sat down on the steps and laughed hysterically. Finally, he said to his amazed companions, "I just thought of the funniest thing that could ever happen."

"What is it?" they asked.

He said, "We left the key in the lobby."

Many people feel as if they have lost the key to getting what they want in life – meaning, happiness, success, peace, security. They have been trudging and toiling at length but feel as if they are locked out of that place they really want to be. They think, "If only I had the key to a whole and happy life!"

That wise and amazing woman Eleanor Roosevelt gave three keys to meaning, happiness, success and peace. "One is that you do whatever comes your way as well as you can," she said. She knew that the key to satisfaction in life is to take pride in whatever you're given to do, regardless how grand or humble the undertaking.

"Another is that you think as little as possible about yourself and as much as possible about other people and about things that are interesting," she continued. Eleanor Roosevelt knew that those who take a genuine interest in the concerns of others and in great ideas lose their desire to worry needlessly about themselves.

"The third is that you receive more joy out of giving joy to others and [that you] should put a good deal of thought into the happiness that you are able to give," she concluded. She was aware that the key to finding happiness is in giving happiness – wherever and whenever possible.

These are three keys that should neither be lost nor locked away in a safe place. Learn to use them – every day – and you'll open doors to those important and wonderful things that will make your life worth living!

P.S.

"Life is no brief candle to me. It is a sort of splendid torch which I have got a hold of for the moment, and I want to make it burn as brightly as possible before handing it on to future generations." ~ *George Bernard Shaw*

Remember

One woman complained to a friend that she couldn't remember anything from one day to the next.

"Let me get this straight," he said. "You can't remember anything from one day to the next. How long has this been going on?"

She said, "How long has what been going on?"

If your memory is not what you would like it to be, it may help to focus on the few things you really need to remember. This list, compiled from several sources, may just be suitable for framing.

- Remember that your presence is a present to the world.
- Remember that you are a unique and unrepeatable creation.
- Remember that your life can be what you want it to be.

34

- Remember to take the days just one at a time.
- Remember to count your blessings, not your troubles.
- Remember that you'll make it through whatever comes along.
- Remember that most of the answers you need are within you.
- Remember those dreams waiting to be realized.
- Remember that decisions are too important to leave to chance.
- Remember to always reach for the best that is within you.
- Remember that nothing wastes more energy than worry.
- Remember that not getting what you want is sometimes a wonderful stroke of luck.
- Remember that the longer you carry a grudge, the heavier it gets.
- Remember not to take things too seriously.
- Remember to laugh.
- Remember that a little love goes a long way.
- Remember that a lot goes forever.
- Remember that happiness is more often found in giving than getting.
- Remember that life's treasures are people, not things.
- Remember that miracles still happen.

So You Made A Mistake?

The obituary editor of a city newspaper was not one who would admit his mistakes easily. One day, he got a phone call from an irate subscriber who complained that her name just appeared in the obituary column. "Really?" was the calm reply. "Where are you calling from?"

There is no shame in making mistakes. They are an important and necessary part of learning.

A young man came in for an interview with his manager. "Tell me," the young man asked her, "how did you become so successful?"

"Two words," she said.

"And what are they?"

"Right decisions."

He asked, "How did you make right decisions?"

"One word – experience."

"And how did you get experience?"

"Two words," she said.

"And what are they?"

36

"Wrong decisions."

In order to profit from our mistakes, we have to get out and make some. And so long as we keep making different ones each time, we're learning and growing!

Are you feeling badly about a mistake you recently made? Then decide what you will do differently next time, make amends if necessary, forgive yourself and move on.

Are you afraid of taking a necessary risk for fear of making a mistake? Remember, even poor choices can be marvelous opportunities for learning. For it is through those wrong decisions that we will learn to make right decisions.

So make those mistakes. Make them boldly! In the end, they will make you better. And if you make enough, you'll become the best you can be!

P.S.

There are two rules for success:
  1. *Never tell everything you know.*
  2. *See rule # 1.*

Just A Dime

Can one dime make a difference? Here is a woman who turned a dime into millions of dollars.

Her name was Martha Berry. This clever woman founded the Berry School in Rome, Georgia. She scraped together funds from every source possible. One day she approached Henry Ford, of Ford automobile fame, and asked for a contribution. Patronizingly, he reached into his pocket and pulled out a dime.

Rather than be insulted or discouraged by the "gift," Miss Berry bought a package of seed peanuts with it. The seeds were planted and tended, and they eventually yielded a large crop, which she later sold.

Again she called on Mr. Ford. "Here's the dime you gave me last year," she said, handing him a coin. Then she told him of the return she had realized from his token investment.

Ford was so impressed that, in the years to come, he gave millions of dollars to the school.

39

Can one dime make a difference? Yes, if we invest it well.

How about one hour of your time? Can it make a difference? Or how about the life of one person? Can a life like yours or mine *really* make a difference? The answer to each of these questions is the same: Yes, if we invest it well.

Now...how are your investments doing?

The Push You Need

Author and speaker Tony Robbins teaches that we are each motivated both by pain and by pleasure. We can change behaviors and attitudes as we utilize the pain and pleasure principles.

Here is how it works: One of the most successful American football coaches was Vince Lombardi. But he was not an easy coach to play for. One player, Henry Jordan, chuckled about Lombardi, "He treats us all the same – like dogs." He went on to say, "I play for the love of the game, the love of the money and the fear of Lombardi."

When he plays for the love of the game and the love of the money, he is motivated by pleasure. He thinks of the enjoyment he will get when he is on the field and his financial success as a professional player. He may even think of the personal recognition he receives as a professional player and the feelings of self-respect he experiences as he continues to succeed. The pleasure of these thoughts motivates him to play well.

41

When he thinks of Lombardi's ire if he does less than his best, he is motivated by pain. Fear is emotional pain – as real as any physical pain. He may think also of the pain of losing his position to another player or even of the embarrassment of a fumbled ball. All of these "pain thoughts" help him to rise to his best level of performance. We will go to great lengths to avoid pain, in whatever form we find it.

What do you need motivation to do? Is it something related to your job or school? Or something personal, such as a physical or emotional change? Or do you need more encouragement to develop a certain personality trait or to pursue a goal you have neglected far too long?

Utilize the principles of pain and pleasure. Think of the pain you will eventually feel (or even feel now!) as you fail to follow your heart's lead. Be creative. Then think of the pleasure you will experience as you do or become whatever it is you want for yourself. Let these thoughts serve as the impetus to move out into the exciting new directions you have plotted for yourself.

Pain and pleasure are part of our daily lives. Use these feelings and you will find the push you need to give birth to your beautiful dreams!

P.S.

The three stages in a man's life:
1. He believes in Santa Claus.
2. He doesn't believe in Santa Claus.
3. He is Santa Claus.
One reader wrote that actually there is another stage:
4. He looks like Santa Claus!

Setting Your Outlook

A man who fell off a skyscraper was heard to say as he passed the 12th floor, "So far, so good!" One might say he was an optimist.

I believe in optimism. I believe that there is great power in an optimistic attitude, especially when it is grounded in reality.

The late Brian Johnston, a well-known British broadcaster, demonstrated the power of an optimistic outlook. He delighted millions of listeners with his radio programs. He was also a top-class cricket commentator and enthusiast for the game. He once said, "I am a great optimist. Every time I go to a cricket match, I think it is going to be the best game I have ever seen. Of course, it never is, but what pleasure it gives me in anticipation!"

Is he simply playing silly mind games? I don't think so. Imagine how much more we might enjoy a meal, a book, an outing, a concert, a holiday – if we think these just may be the best we have

44

ever experienced! A strong, positive outlook can make all the difference. The poet writes:

"One ship sails east, the other west
On the self-same winds that blow.
'Tis the set of the sails and not the gales
That determines the way she goes."

Set your mental outlook to always expect the best. You will often get exactly what you expect! And even if you don't, you will still get to enjoy the pleasure of anticipation.

[Thanks to Ron Coston for his information about Brian Johnston.]

Your Most Valued Strength

I learned of a research organization that asked several thousand people, "What are the most serious faults of executives in dealing with their associates and subordinates?" Several could be chosen. What do you think was mentioned most often? Here is the list:

- *15% Bias and letting emotions rule.*
- *15% Indecision.*
- *21% Miscellaneous; including lack of courtesy, sarcasm, jealousy, nervousness and loss of temper.*
- *17% Failure to delegate authority.*
- *17% Arrogance.*
- *17% Arbitrariness.*
- *19% Lack of frankness and sincerity.*
- *24% Lack of leadership.*
- *34% Failure to size up employees correctly.*
- *36% Failure to show appreciation or give credit.*

46

- *68% Failure to see the other person's point of view.*

The fault cited most often, as the survey shows, was failure to see the other person's point of view. It was mentioned nearly twice as often as the next most common problem.

On a more positive side, the strength most valued in the workplace is the ability to understand another. And I suspect that strength rates high in all relationships. We don't always need others in our life to agree with us, but we do need to feel heard and understood. In fact, feeling understood may well be one of our greatest emotional needs. Without it, we can feel disheartened, we believe we don't matter and we find ourselves increasingly unhappy and lonely.

Grade school children demonstrate this important human need to be heard. One writer tells about a group of children who seldom talked about personal problems with their teachers or the school principal for fear of the consequences. But...in which of the adults at school were the children confiding most often? The school custodian! Here was a person who would listen without judging. Here was someone safe, someone who would understand.

Author Og Mandino gives us this challenge: "Beginning today, treat everyone you meet as if they were going to be dead by midnight. Extend to

47

them all the care, kindness, and understanding you can muster, and do it with no thought of any reward. Your life will never be the same again."

It's a universal principle: when we habitually decide to be understanding, we soon feel more understood. And our lives are never the same again.

P.S.

"I've tried and tried to put my thumb on it, but perhaps the problem is bigger than my thumb."

49

What Do You Need?

Do you know what you really need? I'm not talking about material things. I mean, what do you need to make your life all you want it to be?

Author Stephen Covey says that people all share four basic needs: the need to live, to love, to learn and to leave a legacy.

We need to live. Not just to breathe but to live life fully. Dr. Philip Humbert asks, "What remarkable, extraordinary and amazing things will you do with this wild and wonderful miracle, your one and only life?"

We need to love. We also need to be loved. As anthropologist Margaret Mead puts it, "One of the oldest human needs is having someone wonder where you are when you don't come home at night."

We need to learn. And not only for a few years when we are young. We must be life-long learners who never stop growing, never cease to improve. For when we no longer grow, we stagnate. And when we stagnate, we die.

Finally, we need to leave a legacy. It is a basic desire to want our lives to count for something. In the words of Ralph Waldo Emerson: "To laugh often and much; to win the respect of intelligent people and affection of children; to earn the appreciation of honest critics and endure the betrayal of false friends; to appreciate beauty; to find the best in others; to leave the world a little bit better, whether by a healthy child, a garden patch or a redeemed social condition; to know even one life has breathed easier because you have lived. This is to have succeeded."

These are four needs that must never be neglected. Live fully, love completely, learn constantly and leave something worthwhile behind. It is the path to success. And to joy.

When Disaster Looms

It's said that we are regularly faced with magnificent opportunities brilliantly disguised as impossible situations. I once read of a quick-thinking salesperson who uncovered such an opportunity which seemed, at first, to be a disaster.

With the presses set to run three million copies of Theodore Roosevelt's 1912 convention speech, the publisher discovered that permission had not been obtained to use photos of Roosevelt and his running mate, Governor Hiram Johnson of California. Copyright law put the penalty for such oversights at one dollar per copy.

Spotting a hidden opportunity, the chairperson of the campaign committee dictated a telegram to the Chicago studio that had taken the pictures: "Planning to issue three million copies of Roosevelt speech with pictures of Roosevelt and Johnson on cover. Great publicity opportunity for photographers. What will you pay us to use your photographs?"

52

The reply came back: "Appreciate opportunity, but can only pay $250." The campaign committee avoided a three-million-dollar fine and came out $250 ahead!

Was the oversight a disaster or an opportunity? The answer, of course, depended on how they approached the problem. Perhaps that is why the Chinese word for "crisis" is written using the characters for "danger" and "opportunity." With a cool head and a little imagination, the danger in a crisis may be turned into an unexpected opportunity.

What hopeless problem are you currently facing? And what might happen if you approach it as a magnificent opportunity brilliantly disguised as an impossible situation?

P.S.

It helps to know the difference between our needs and our wants. As one man says, "Is it a necessity or an accessory?"

Love The Children

Felice R. Prager writes in *Reader's Digest* (August, 1999) that the kids had been driving her nuts, asking her to buy them a talking bird, until she finally got them a parrot. They named him Wilbur and tried to teach him some words, but all he would say was, "Hello. Hello." Her oldest son Jeff worked with Wilbur, trying to get him to say, "Jeff is the greatest." Nothing.

Her husband tried. "Give this guy a raise," he repeated. Nothing.

Felice took a turn. "Clean your room." Still nothing.

Finally, Wilbur started talking. During dinner all they heard was: "He did it. No, he did it." And then, "Get out of my room!"

Hers is not the only house where those words are repeated like a childhood mantra! My heart goes out to parents. Like the father who lamented, "When I was a child, I never gave any thought to running away from home. But now that I am a parent, I think about it all the time."

Some advice I heard several years ago has inspired me to constantly give my best to my children. The advice, surprisingly, came from someone who was not a parent at all, but rather a nun. It was offered by Mother Teresa shortly after she made a speech about her work with the sick and dying and her efforts to help orphans in India. Following her address, a member of the audience stood and asked, "You have done so much to make the world a better place. What can we do?" He clearly wanted to assist in her work.

Mother Teresa smiled and said simply, "Love your children."

The questioner looked perplexed and seemed about to speak again when Mother Teresa raised her hand. "There are other things you can do," she said, "but that is the best. Love your children. Love your children as much as you can. That is the best."

I can't help but believe that her advice, if followed by all parents and all adults in all places at all times, will transform our world in a generation. Just love the children – all the children. Love them as much as you can. That is best.

Letting Go Of Success!

I want to make the most of every day. And, like most people, I've discovered that the best way to do it is to let go of past failures.

But that's not all. One can never fully enjoy today while dwelling too much on past successes, either. People never succeed while resting comfortably on their laurels. As Ivern Ball has said, "The past should be a springboard, not a hammock." The fact is, sometimes our successes hold us back more than our failures!

I once heard a story about the actor Clark Gable. A friend paid Gable a visit one afternoon at the actor's home. She brought along her small son, who amused himself by playing with toy cars on the floor. He pretended he was racing those cars around a great track, which in reality was an imaginary circle around a golden statuette. The small statue the boy played with was actually the Oscar Clark Gable won for his performance in the 1934 movie *It Happened One Night.*

57

When his mother told him the time had come to leave, the little boy asked the actor, "Can I have this?" pointing to the Oscar.

"Sure," he smiled. "It's yours."

The horrified mother objected. "Put that back immediately!"

Giving the child the golden statue, Clark Gable said, "Having the Oscar around doesn't mean anything to me; earning it does." The actor seemed to know that past success could be a comfortable hammock upon which he may be tempted to rest, rather than a springboard launching him to the next level.

Biblical wisdom says, "Do not cling to events of the past or dwell on what happened long ago." You may have learned to let go of past failures and mistakes in order to free the present. But will you loosen your grip on past successes and achievements in order to free the future? Will your past be a springboard or a restful hammock?

"I like the dreams of the future better than the history of the past," said Thomas Jefferson. I agree. After all, the future, not the past, is where the rest of your life will be lived.

P.S.

"Enjoy the little things in life, for one day you may look back and realize they were the big things." ~ Antonio Smith

Hurry Up And Be Patient!

You've heard it said, "Hurry up and wait!" But learning to wait calmly is an important part of living. In this age of high-speed connections and instantaneous results, it helps to remember that the Mayflower made its historic voyage across the Atlantic Ocean at about two miles per hour! How did those early settlers occupy their time as they were waiting to arrive?

I love the story of a passenger on Britain's Imperial Airways, a company that pioneered air travel between England and Australia in the mid-1930s. "If you have time to spare, go by air," was the popular expression of the day. Airliners were both slow and incapable of flying long distances.

One of the very first flights took off from Croydon Airport near London and flew to northern France where it was delayed extensively due to bad weather. When it arrived in the south of France, one of the motors had failed and it was necessary to wait for another engine to be shipped by sea from Eng-

60

land. There were further lengthy delays along the route in Rome, Cairo, the Middle East, etc., until finally the flight had progressed as far as Singapore.

At this point a lady passenger asked the manager in Singapore if he thought the flight would arrive in Australia in the next few weeks because she was expecting a baby shortly.

"My dear lady," he replied, "you should never have commenced your trip in that condition."

She replied, "I didn't."

Next time you miss a flight, think about her predicament and "hurry up and be patient"! The sooner you're patient, the easier your life will become. When you're patient, you can relax and enjoy the ride.

There is great benefit in learning to wait calmly and creatively. Here is a "waiting checklist" to test your waiting skills:

- Do you expect delays, or do they catch you unawares? Do you anticipate those times when you are likely to have to wait?
- Do you calmly let your inner motor idle though others around you may be stripping their gears?
- Do you welcome unexpected delays as a gift of time, which can be used creatively? Do you use the free time to plan ahead or qui-

etly meditate (to get in touch with your soul)?

- Do you prepare for delays? Do you have work or entertainment handy when forced to wait?

How did you do on the exercise? Are you making the most of your waiting time? We will never escape delays, but we can use them creatively. Now is the time to hurry up and be patient!

Act Two

The date is June 24, 1859. Suddenly, there he is, atop a hill overlooking the plain of Solferino. Napoleon's troops prepare for battle with the Austrians below, and Henri Dunant has a box-seat view from his place on the hill.

Trumpets blare, muskets crack and cannons boom. The two armies crash into each other, as Henri looks on, transfixed. He sees the dust rising. He hears the screams of the injured. He watches bleeding, maimed men take their last breaths as he stares in horror at the scene below.

Henri doesn't mean to be there. He is only on a business trip – to speak to Napoleon III about a financial transaction between the Swiss and the French. But he arrived late and now finds himself in a position to witness first-hand the atrocities of war.

What Henri sees from his hill, however, pales in comparison with what he is soon to witness. Entering a small town shortly after the fierce encounter, Henri now observes the battle's refugees.

Every building is filled with the mangled, the injured, the dead. Henri, aching with pity, decides to stay in the village three more days to comfort the young soldiers.

He realizes that his life will never be the same again. Driven by a powerful passion to abolish war, Henri Dunant will eventually lose his successful banking career and all his worldly possessions only to die as a virtual unknown in an obscure poorhouse.

But we remember Henri today because he was the first recipient of the Nobel Peace Prize (in 1901). We also remember him because of the movement he founded – the Red Cross.

Act One of Henri Dunant's life closed June 24, 1859. Act Two opened immediately and played the remainder of his 81 years.

Many people's lives can be divided into Act One and Act Two. The first performance ends when one decides to ultimately follow a new direction or passion. Henri Dunant's old life, driven by financial success, prestige and power, no longer satisfied. A new Henri Dunant emerged in Act Two; one who was motivated by love, compassion and an overriding commitment to abolish the horrors of war.

For some, Act Two may begin with a conversion, or a turning point. Others speak of a defining moment. However it is understood, the "old self" is laid to rest and a new self is born – one governed by principle, spirit and passion.

You may be ready for Act Two. It may be the next scene of a life that counts.

P.S.

"The word 'no' carries a lot more meaning when spoken by a parent who also knows how to say 'yes.'" ~ Joyce Maynard

Imperturbability

I think Charles Allen said it first. "When faced with problems which threaten to steal your peace of mind, learn the meaning of the word 'imperturbability.'"

I heard of two artists who were asked to illustrate peace. Each was assigned the task of depicting a peaceful scene on canvas.

The first artist drew a beautiful picture of a countryside on a warm, spring day. A soft sun illumines green grass and bathes a picturesque farmhouse and grazing cattle in its warmth. A farmer walks contentedly behind strong plow horses preparing his field for spring planting. The picture is one of beauty and quiet tranquility.

The other artist took a different approach. He drew a majestic, rugged cliff. Gnarled trees, twisted by years of violent winds, jut from the craggy mountainside. Dark clouds hang low and fierce while jagged streaks of lightening slash

67

across an angry sky. The picture is one of violence, chaos and rage.

But as one looks closely, something else becomes visible. There in one of the crevices of the rocky mountain, tucked back just out of reach of the wind and rain – a nest with two small birds. Apparently unconcerned about the impending storm, they appear calm, cozy and peaceful as they patiently wait for the turbulence to pass.

And isn't that the way it so often is? We may want to be surrounded by peace, but storms rage. Problems and pressures without threaten to steal peace of mind within.

The answer is imperturbability: inner peace that doesn't leave when circumstances change. It's a peace that is greater than the problems of life, built on assurance that the tempest will finally pass, that we will survive the storm, that we may grow stronger because of it and, in the meantime, we will not endure it alone.

Imperturbability – it's the result of a peace that passes understanding. For serenity is not freedom from the storm, but peace amid the storm.

When You've Been "Throwed"

It is well said: "Strength and courage aren't always measured in medals and victories. They are measured in the struggles we overcome. The strongest people aren't always the people who win but the people who don't give up when they lose."

It's been said that Andrew Jackson's boyhood friends just couldn't understand how he became a famous general and then the President of the United States. They knew of others who had greater talent but who never succeeded. One of Jackson's friends commented, "Why, Jim Brown, who lived right down the pike from Jackson, was not only smarter, but he could throw Andy three times out of four in a wrestling match. But look where Andy is now."

Another friend responded, "How did there happen to be a fourth time? Don't they usually say three times and out?"

"Sure, they were supposed to, but not Andy. He would never admit he was beat – he would never stay 'throwed.' Jim Brown would get tired, and on the fourth try Andy would throw him and be the winner."

Andrew Jackson just wouldn't stay "throwed"! And that determination served him well for many years.

Life will knock us off our feet again and again. You've been there and so have I. But some people just won't stay "throwed." They get up again, dust themselves off and go for it one more time. These are people of courage. They are also people of faith and hope.

Maybe you have been knocked off your feet. Will you stay "throwed," or will you rise and give it your best one more time?

P.S.

The younger we are, the more we want to change the world. The older we are, the more we want to change the young....

Get Some Altitude

I heard of a tornado that recently ripped through the central part of Oklahoma. Guy, a church pastor, and his wife, Vickie, lived directly in the path of the on-coming storm. They took refuge in a closet in the parsonage.

Guy belongs to a denomination (United Methodist), which is known for moving its pastors frequently, and he was scheduled for a move to a new parish in June. Furthermore, as a church leader, he no doubt encountered any number of storms and conflicts among church members. But a tornado was something else entirely, and hiding in the closet seemed the best course of action for the couple.

After the tornado passed, they emerged from their hiding place and were astonished to discover that their closet was the only part of the house left standing! Though they lost everything, they had come through unscathed. As the couple stood in the middle of the debris that used to be their home,

72

Vickie's first comment was: "Wow, Guy! This is wonderful! This will be the easiest move we've ever made!"

Here is a person who knows something about handling difficulties. Sometimes we have to look beyond a problem before we can move forward.

If you have ever flown in a jet on a foggy or cloudy day, you probably know something about looking beyond problems. All seems dark and dreary on the ground. Yet every day is a sunny day if we can only get enough altitude.

Thomas Carlyle put it like this: "What you can see, yet cannot see over, is as good as infinite." Get some altitude and you will be able to see beyond the problem!

Finer Than Wealth

I love the story about an angel who suddenly appears at a faculty meeting and tells the dean of the college that, in return for his unselfish and exemplary behavior, he will be given his choice of infinite wealth, wisdom or beauty. Without hesitating, the dean selects infinite wisdom.

"Done!" says the angel, and disappears in a cloud of smoke and a bolt of lightning.

Now, all heads turn toward the dean, who sits surrounded by a faint halo of light. At length, one of his colleagues whispers, "Say something."

The dean looks at them and says, "I should have taken the money."

Though wealth is highly regarded in our world, I rather suspect this fictitious academic made the better choice. Wisdom, like many other virtues, is usually more difficult to obtain and can be far more satisfying.

I've heard it said that when our hearts are empty, we collect "things." On the other hand,

74

when our hearts are full, we tend to lose interest in most of the "stuff" of life. The "things of the heart" become all important. Things like love and joy and peace. Or wisdom. Or hope. Or faith.

And the wonderful truth is that these gifts are given freely to any who will take them! None of us has to live without love. There really is joy to be found in this life. And we can know peace – now.

Fra Giovanni gave us these immortal words in 1513:

"No heaven can come to us unless our hearts find rest in today. Take heaven!
No peace lies in the future that is not hidden in his present moment. Take peace!
The gloom of this world is but a shadow.
Behind it, yet within reach, is joy.
There is a radiance and glory in the darkness, could we but see, and to see we have only to look. I beseech you to look.
Life is so generous a giver...."

You have already been offered things even finer than infinite wealth. Will you grasp them and make them yours – today?

75

P.S.

"Life is like pudding. It takes both the salt and the sugar to make a good one." ~ Old New England proverb

Ain't Nothing You Can Do

Jewish humor has it that a rookie recruit for the New York City Police had passed all of his examinations except public health. The police surgeon said, "Well, Murphy, you've done very well. I'll ask you one question and if you do all right on that, you can become a cop."

He wanted to ask him how he would respond if a rabid dog bit somebody; for instance, what does he know about the disease, how would he treat the victim, whom would he call and so forth. The doctor said, "Now, tell me, what is rabies, and what are you going to do about it?"

"Well, Captain," Murphy replied, "rabies is Jewish priests, and there ain't nothin' you can do about it."

There "ain't nothin' you can do" about quite a few situations! And it's true with people, too. There ain't nothin' you can do about the way they are, so it is fruitless to try to change them into something else. You are wise to learn to accept

77

them without conditions, understand them the best you can and love them anyway. For they probably won't change much and there just ain't nothin' you can do about it.

Sam Keen Christine said, "We come to love, not by finding a perfect person, but by learning to see an imperfect person perfectly." It's all about acceptance.

What We See

A long time ago a baby was born to poor parents. His future looked bleak as he grew to see a life of dreariness and poverty before him. He joined the army as a common soldier and was wounded so severely that he never regained the use of his left arm.

He later failed to find decent employment and, on two occasions, was sent to debtor's prison. He continued to have brushes with the law and struggled just to survive.

But, despite the severity of his life, he never let go of his dream...to write a book. He wrote that book and in it he told a beautiful story which welled from his heart's deepest dreams and yearnings. It has moved generations of people the world over ever since. It is about a man who saw the world differently than everyone else. Though created in suffering, the book is an inspiring tale of irrepressible hope. This man's story has been put to music and film, translated into numerous languages and remains a literary classic after some 400 years.

The author was Miguel de Cervantes Saavedra and the book is *Don Quioxote De La Mancha.*

Perhaps Cervantes himself believed, as did his character, that the world "sees people as they are – I see them as they can be!" For Cervantes may never have accomplished such a magnificent work had he not seen some potential within himself that was hidden from the rest of the world. He knew, and has taught others ever since, that great truth: What we see will come to be.

Some see situations as they are, others as they can be. Some see people as they are, others as they can be. And some see themselves as they are, others as they can be.

But when we look beyond the present reality, dismal as it may seem, and set our sights upon the best that is within a situation or a human being, then, too, what we see will come to be. And we'll know the power of hope.

P.S.

"Courage is being scared to death but saddling up anyway." ~ John Wayne

Got A Problem?

Do you have a problem? Does it seem like it just won't go away? Perhaps a little more creativity is all that is needed. Let me explain.

Thomas Edison has been credited with inventing the first half of the twentieth century. And certainly one of his greatest inventions was the incandescent electric light bulb. But Edison takes no credit for making the light bulb available to the world. He was simply an inventor.

Edison's bulb did not burn for long; it gave off little light and it was too expensive. A man named William David Coolidge spent seven years improving the light bulb to make it more practical. Largely because of his work, electric light eventually came into common use.

When Coolidge finally succeeded in his efforts, he was questioned about how he was able to make tungsten work. He said, "It was because I was not a metallurgist. Had I been a metallurgist, I would have known that the task was impossible."

82

Henry Ford, too, built his success largely on his ability to "think outside the box." He used to say that he was looking to employ a lot of people "who have an infinite capacity to not know what can't be done." Sometimes, unconventional thinking and a belief that anything is possible are required to solve problems.

You may not be setting out to build a huge company or market a new invention, but you still face difficult problems that beg for creativity. Perhaps you are worried about financing an education. Or you are caring for a loved one with a long-term illness. Or maybe you simply cannot seem to get along with that difficult person you work alongside everyday. These problems, and countless others, just don't seem to go away. Most of us struggle with similar "impossible" situations. If your problem seems impossible, then your usual thinking is probably not working. How can you look at your situation differently? Who can help you consider other solutions and will never tell you that it can't be done? And most important, what would you do if you believed that *anything* were possible? *Anything!*

You may not have succeeded yet because you have become discouraged searching for a solution to your problem. Or perhaps you are not convinced that an answer *can* be found, somehow...somewhere. But a creative and wonderful solution might be just ahead. Look in a different direction. *Find it*! You can...*if* you believe it is there and *if* you believe it can be found.

Today, what would happen if you approached your problem in a new way? Do you want to find out?

The Power Of Solitude

Herman Melville's classic, *Moby Dick*, portrays the whaling industry of his time. In today's world, his book may likely upset readers who share more enlightened attitudes about the use and abuse of animals. But a scene in the story can teach us even today something about the power of solitude and focus in daily life.

Melville gives us a turbulent scene in which a whaleboat scuds across a frothing ocean in pursuit of the great white whale. The sailors are laboring to keep the vessel on course in a raging sea, every muscle taut. They labor furiously as they concentrate on the task at hand. In Captain Ahab's boat, however, there is one man who does nothing. He doesn't hold an oar; he doesn't perspire; he doesn't shout. He is languid – utterly relaxed, quiet and poised. This man is the harpooner, and his job is to patiently wait for the moment. Then Melville gives us this sentence: "To insure the greatest efficiency in the dart, the harpooners of this world must start to their feet out of idleness, and not out of toil."

What a marvelous picture for effective living! Those who would live each day to the fullest must prepare for them from a state of idleness rather than toil. For many people this means a daily period of quiet and meditation to focus, plan or pray.

"I don't have time for that!" some people complain. "My life is simply too busy to add one more thing to it."

But most people find that a regular period of solitude to chart the day's course, still the mind, listen and prepare actually *creates* more time than it *takes*. For we are most effective when we start to our feet out of idleness and not out of toil.

Writer C. S. Lewis put it like this: "The moment you wake up each morning, all your wishes and hopes for the day rush at you like wild animals. And the first job each morning consists in shoving it all back; in listening to that other voice, taking that other point of view, letting that other, larger, stronger, quieter life come flowing in."

If this is not part of your routine, you may be missing out on the best part of the day! Develop the habit of daily solitude and you will be amazed at the difference it can make.

86

P.S.

"The way I see it, if you want the rainbow, you gotta put up with the rain." ~ Dolly Parton

Living In The Same Box

David Wallechinsky in *The Complete Book Of The Olympics* (Penguin Books, 1984) gives us a story that is worth retelling.

It is 1936. American Jesse Owens seems sure to win the long-jump competition in the Olympic games. The previous year he had jumped 26 feet, 8 1/4 inches – a record that will stand for 25 years.

As he walks to the long-jump pit, however, Owens sees a tall, blue-eyed, blond German taking practice jumps in the 26-foot range. Owens feels nervous. He is acutely aware of the Nazis' desire to prove "Aryan superiority." And as a black son of a sharecropper, he knows what it is like to be made to feel inferior.

On his first jump, Owens inadvertently leaps from several inches beyond the takeoff board. Rattled, he fouls on his second attempt, too. One more foul and he will be eliminated.

At this point, the tall German introduces himself as Luz Long. "You should be able to qualify with your eyes closed!" he says to Owens, referring to his upcoming two jumps.

For the next few moments, the African American and the white Nazi chat together. Then Long makes a suggestion. Since the qualifying distance is only 23 feet, 5 1/2 inches, why not make a mark several inches before the takeoff board and jump from there, just to play it safe? Owens does and qualifies easily.

In the finals, Owens sets an Olympic record and earns the second of four gold medals. But who is the first person to congratulate him? Luz Long – in full view of Adolf Hitler.

Owens never again sees Long, who is later killed in World War II. "You could melt down all the medals and cups I have," Owens later writes, "and they wouldn't be a plating on the 24-carat friendship I felt for Luz Long."

Perhaps unknowingly, Luz Long taught the world a valuable lesson.

Someone else put it like this: "We can learn a lot from crayons. Some are sharp...some are pretty...some are dull...some have weird names...and all are different colors.... But they all have to learn to live in the same box."

89

Get Ready!

You heard about the sign posted on a rancher's fence? On the other side of the fence resides the biggest, meanest looking bull you can imagine. The sign is intended to strike fear into the hearts of would-be trespassers. It reads: "Don't attempt to cross this field unless you can do it in 9.9 seconds. The bull can do it in 10 flat!" Don't try to cross that field unless you are prepared! And isn't that the way it is in life? We have to be ready when the opportunity arises or else we will have little chance of success.

Sixth-grade schoolteacher Ms. Shelton believed in readiness. Students remember how she walked in on the first day of class and began writing words of an eighth-grade caliber on the chalkboard. They quickly protested that the words were not on their level and they couldn't learn them.

Their teacher insisted that the students could and would learn these words. She said that she would never teach down to them. Ms. Shelton

90

ended by saying that one of the students in that classroom could go on to greatness, maybe even be president some day, and she wanted to prepare them for that day.

Ms. Shelton spoke those words many years ago. Little did she know that someday one of her students – Jesse Jackson – would take them seriously (*Leadership*, Summer 1992). She believed that if they were well prepared, they could achieve high goals.

Ralph Waldo Emerson once said, "People only see what they are prepared to see." It's also true that they only experience what they are prepared to experience.

"I want to be doing something more significant with my life than what I am doing now," a young man once said to me. Others have lamented, "If only I were involved in a meaningful relationship." And, "If only I could get a better job." You fill in the blanks. What is it you would like to experience that seems to be eluding you? Perhaps the answer is that you are not yet ready. Maybe you need more time to prepare before you are truly ready for that which you desire.

Today is not wasted. If you desire *more* from life, then you can use today as training. For you will experience only what you are prepared to experience. Something wonderful can happen. In the meantime...prepare for that day!

91

P.S.

"I have reached the metallic age...silver in my hair, gold in my teeth and lead in my rear!"

Not Enough To Make A Living

"I don't subscribe to the thesis, 'Let the buyer beware,'" said the American writer Isaac Asimov. "I prefer the disregarded one that goes, 'Let the seller be honest.'"

A century ago, clothier John Wanamaker, whose retail business grew into one of the first department stores, would have agreed. He instilled the attitude of utmost honesty in his employees. The story is told of one of his advertising people who was instructed to make a sign advertising neckties that were reduced in price from one dollar apiece to 25 cents. After personally examining the ties, the adman asked the buyer, "Are they any good?"

"No, they're not," replied the buyer with all sincerity.

The advertiser wanted to be completely honest, so he finally wrote the copy this way: "They are not as good as they look, but they are good enough at 25 cents." The department sold out of ties almost immediately and was forced to purchase several more weeks' supply of cheap ties to fill the persistent demand (*Selling Solutions,* Juanita Ruiz, Ed., Oct. 1995).

Wanamaker's reputation for honesty helped to later catapult him to the office of U. S. Postmaster General. He believed that only a business based on values has real value. He built his company and his life on his values – and both were successful.

It is truer today than ever before. To be successful, it is not enough to just make a living. We have to make a life. Build your life on solid values and you will build a life of value.

Succeeding At Life

It's said there are three ways to get to the top of a tree: climb it, sit on an acorn or make friends with a big bird. But I suspect that only one of those options is worth considering.

Likewise, there may be many ways to climb to the top of an organization or to reach whatever heights capture your imagination. But I believe there is only one way to truly succeed at living.

How? It has to do with the word "priorities."

Success at life may not always mean getting to the top. But it does mean finding joy and peace of mind. It means having dreams and pursuing them. And it means setting worthwhile priorities. Succeeding at living is important to anybody who wants to live as fully and joyously as possible.

American football coaching legend Vince Lombardi can help. He is often credited with saying, "Winning isn't everything, it's the only thing." Lombardi's dream was to coach a winning team, but it's a mistake to think that a winning team was

95

his greatest goal. He felt it was more important to succeed at life.

How did he do it? Few people know that winning football games wasn't "the only thing" to Lombardi. He actually listed his life priorities in this order: God, his family and his career.

He knew what was important. And he knew that keeping his priorities straight could bring him joy, peace and, ultimately, success. Which made him a winner – at life.

P.S.

When in charge, ponder. When in trouble, delegate. When in doubt, mumble.

Building Your Trust Fund

The young parents paid the baby-sitter and dropped her off at her home. As she turned to leave, she said, "By the way, I promised Amy that if she went to bed, you'd buy her a pony in the morning." Ouch.... (I understand that she is looking for a new sitting job.)

Parents, of course, want their children to trust them, so they try to keep their promises. By modeling trust, they hope to teach their children to also be trustworthy. But keeping faith with others needn't be limited solely to the family. There are few elements in *any* relationship more important than trust.

Motivational speaker Matt Dimaio equates having someone's trust to having money in the bank. Just like a bank account, we must make deposits if we expect to make withdrawals. When we keep our word, it's like making a deposit into our trust fund. The more often we perform the way we promised, the larger our balance will be. Whenever

98

we break our word, we have made a withdrawal from our account.

Dimaio tells us that we have a separate trust fund with each person with whom we have a relationship. If we have been making regular deposits into our account with that individual, when the time comes that we are unable to keep our word (let's face it, nobody's perfect!), we will still have a large enough balance of trust to cover the debt. That person will realize that our account is still good. We are trustworthy!

Scottish writer George MacDonald said, "To be trusted is a greater compliment than to be loved." Whether or not that is true, I would rather have a healthy emotional trust fund than a large bank account. Trust is more valuable than money – it's the stuff great relationships are built of.

A Life That Counts

They said he died!

One morning in 1888, Alfred Nobel, inventor of dynamite, the man who had spent his life amassing a fortune from the manufacture and sale of weapons of destruction, awoke to read his own obituary. Of course, it was a mistake. Alfred's brother had died, and the reporter inadvertently wrote Alfred's obituary.

For the first time, Alfred Nobel saw himself as the world saw him – "the dynamite king," the great industrialist who had made an immense fortune from explosives. This, as far as the general public was concerned, was the entire purpose of his life. None of his true intentions surfaced. Nothing was said about his work to break down the barriers that separated persons and ideas. He was, quite simply, a merchant of death, and for that alone would he be remembered.

Alfred read the obituary with horror. He felt that the world must know the true meaning and pur-

100

pose of his life! He resolved to do this through his last will and testament. The final disposition of his fortune would show the world his life's ideals. And at that time came into being yearly prizes for chemistry, physics, medicine, literature – and the famous Nobel Peace Prize.

If you were to read your own obituary today, what would it say? Do others know what you stand for, what you believe in and what truly matters to you?

Dr. Philip Humbert asks, "What remarkable, extraordinary and amazing things will you do with this wild and wonderful miracle, your one and only life?" The question should perhaps also be asked this way: "What will you do with this wild and wonderful miracle, your one and only *day*?" For how we spend our days will decide how we spend our lives.

Chances are, you will not be reading your own obituary. But you have already begun to write it – day by day, moment by moment. Live your todays as if they truly matter, and tomorrow you will look back on a life that counted.

P.S.

"Technological society has succeeded in multiplying the opportunities for pleasure, but it has great difficulty in generating joy." ~ Pope Paul VI

Nothing Is More Important

I sat next to the bed of an old man, a friend for over twenty years, and held his hand. Hal was dying. We both knew these next few days would be his last.

We spent time reminiscing about his long and fruitful career as a church pastor. We talked about old friends. We chatted about his family. And I listened as he offered sage wisdom and advice to a member of a "younger generation."

At a lull in the conversation, Hal seemed to carefully consider what he was about to say next. Then he squeezed my hand, gazed intently into my eyes and whispered, just loud enough for me to hear, "Nothing is more important than relationships." I knew that this was somehow near the pinnacle of his life's learnings. As he considered all of his experiences – personal, professional, spiritual and family – this one ultimate observation surfaced above the rest: "Nothing is more important than relationships."

"Don't get overly caught up in your career," he seemed to be saying to me. "Likewise, don't use people in order to achieve your goals, then throw them away. No project, no program, no task should be pursued at the expense of friends and family. Remember," I heard him saying, as clearly as if he were speaking the words, "that in the end, only your relationships will truly matter. Tend them well."

Writer Og Mandino puts it this way: "Beginning today," he said, "treat everyone you meet as if he or she were going to be dead by midnight. Extend to them all the care, kindness and understanding you can muster, and do so with no thought of any reward. Your life will never be the same again."

At the end of a long life, my friend Hal would have agreed.

Relax

Did you know that practicing some form of daily relaxation is one of the greatest gifts you can give yourself? Taking a few minutes each day to quiet your mind and breathe deeply can make a big difference in how you feel throughout your day and into the night.

We're told that the word "relax" has its origin in the Latin word "relaxare," which means "to loosen." When we relax, we are in effect loosening tension, releasing tightly held energy and letting go. From the state of relaxation we can experience calm peacefulness.

Relaxation also means taking regular time off work. Extended periods of rest are a biological necessity. The human body is like an old-fashioned wind-up clock. If it is not rewound by relaxing every few days, ultimately it will run itself down.

A group of Americans made a trip with Brazilian natives down the Amazon River. The first day they rushed. The second day they rushed. The next day they rushed. One day, anxious to continue the trek, they were surprised to find the natives seated together in a circle.

When asked the reason for the delay, a guide answered, "They are waiting. They cannot move further until their souls have caught up with their bodies."

Do you owe yourself time to let your soul catch up with your body?

P.S.

"Stop worrying about the potholes in the road and enjoy the journey." ~ Babs Hoffman

The Best Revenge

As the story goes, a group of occupational soldiers hired a local boy to run errands for them. The soldiers liked to relieve stress by playing practical jokes on the young boy. They would hide his belongings, put gum in his shoes, or send him on silly errands.

The boy handled the joking quite well. He never seemed upset by it. After a while, the soldiers decided that they had bothered the child enough. They approached him to apologize and to tell him that they would no longer play any jokes on him.

The boy replied in stilted English, "You stop making joke on me, I stop spitting in your soup."

He had his revenge. But for most of us, revenge turns out to be more bitter than sweet. It "has no more quenching effect on emotions than salt water has on thirst," one writer says. And it's true. The desire to inflict hurt and pain remains long after one has given in to the urge to get even. Bitter emotions are more often quenched by love and understanding than by fighting back.

Over 400 years ago, the English poet George Herbert said, "Living well is the best revenge." Good advice – especially when tempted to get even.

Into The Wilderness

A young reporter wanted to get a feel for agriculture, so he called upon a farmer and said, "How's your wheat coming along?"

The farmer replied, "I didn't plant any."

"Really?" asked the reporter. "I thought this was supposed to be wheat country."

"Some say it is," came the reply. "But I was afraid we might not see enough rain this year."

"Well, what about your corn. How is it doing?" the young man inquired.

"Didn't plant corn this year," the farmer said. "I was afraid of corn blight."

"Alfalfa?"

"Nope. Afraid the price might drop."

"Well, then," asked the reporter, "what did you plant?"

"Nothin'," the farmer said. "I just played it safe."

Sir High Walpole advised, "Don't play for safety – it's the most dangerous thing in the world."

110

Of course, unnecessary risk-taking is foolish. But if life is to be lived fully, then saying *no* to fear and taking that risk may be a necessary step to success.

It takes courage to do what you've never done and go where you've never been. Whatever huge decision looms before you, your best solution will likely be made from the side of courage, rather than fear; for in the end, a fearful decision is a dangerous decision.

Alan Alda puts it like this: "You have to leave the city of your comfort and go into the wilderness of your intuition. You can't get there by bus, only by hard work, risking, and by not quite knowing what you're doing. What you'll discover will be wonderful – yourself."

Does that sound like a place you want to go?

P.S.

"I don't have to attend every argument I'm invited to." ~ Anonymous

Call Me Crazy

Bangkok television used to air the American situation comedy *LaVerne and Shirley*. For whatever reason, officials there believed that a disclaimer was necessary for the Thailand audience, so this subtitle was added to each episode: "The two women depicted in the following episode are from an insane asylum."

Personally, I'm thankful there is a little craziness in the world! And I don't mind not acting like everybody else. Like the "irrepressible" Leo Buscaglia once said: "I don't mind if people think I'm crazy. In fact, I think it's great! It gives me tremendous latitude for behavior."

It may seem like craziness to most people, but I try to be *joyful* whenever possible. I believe that a joyful response is, more than anything, a habit, just as fear and worry are life-long habits. And maybe I can't be happy or rejoice *for* all things, but more and more, I'd like to learn to rejoice *in* all things.

113

Like pleasure. There are too few opportunities for hearty laughter, so none should be passed up! I don't want to take the good that happens for granted.

And, if possible, I want to feel genuine happiness about those ordinary things and events that make up most of our days. The happier I am with everyday duties and responsibilities, the more grateful I am just to be alive.

But finally, I want to learn to be happy even in those difficult and trying times. I won't be happy *for* them (who likes problems?), just *in* them. I need the soothing medicine of laughter when it hurts. I also know that at the other end of my problem is a lesson – I'll emerge wiser, or maybe stronger, or perhaps a better person in any number of ways for having faced it successfully.

So call me crazy, but I want to learn to rejoice in all things. And I am just crazy enough to think it's possible!

This Wondrous World

Not everyone has a good grip of science. But these children's scientific musings at least show humor and creativity!

To explain nuclear reactions, one child said, "When they broke open molecules, the found they were only stuffed with atoms. But when they broke open atoms, they found them stuffed with explosions."

Concerning astronomy, one child said, "Most books now say our sun is a star. But it still knows how to change back into a sun in the daytime." And another said, "Some people can tell what time it is by looking at the sun. But I have never been able to make out the numbers."

"Vacuums are nothings," said a young physics student. "We only mention them to let them know we know they're there."

"Evaporation gets blamed for a lot of things people forget to put the top on," one child observed.

"Rain is often known as soft water, oppositely known as hail," reported a budding meteorologist. Another added, "Thunder is a rich source of loudness."

Other children added these observations: "Isotherms and isobars are even more important than their names sound." And, "It is so hot in some places that the people there have to live in other places." And, "The wind is like the air, only pushier."

These children have a way to go in their quest for more knowledge, but I applaud their efforts to learn more about the universe. Unfortunately, the reputation of science suffers in some circles. There are those who feel that a scientific mindset and a spiritual outlook are contrary to one another. They believe that facts revealed by science contradict spiritual truths. Not so!

William Bragg, a pioneer in the field of X-ray crystallography, made the point quite succinctly. He was asked whether science and theology are opposed to one another. "Yes, but in the sense that my thumb and forefinger are opposed to one another – between science and theology, we cannot grasp everything, but surely the combination reveals more of the cosmic mystery than either can touch alone." They *need* each other.

If you love the universe – if you love life, then learn about it. Learn about it from every place possible. Learn from science. Learn from the spiritual disciplines. Learn and keep an open mind, for that is the only way to truth. And the more you learn, the more you'll discover that there is nothing so enchanting or wondrous as this world in which we live!

P.S.

Recognize joy when it arrives in the plain brown wrappings of everyday life.

You Are "A People"

A little girl was asked to bring her birth certificate to school one day. Her mother wisely cautioned her about the important document and told her to be especially careful with it. But in spite of her good intentions, the child lost it. When she became aware of its loss, she began to cry.

"What's the problem, Honey?" her teacher asked sympathetically.

The little girl wailed, "I lost my excuse for being born!"

Isn't it wonderful that we don't need an excuse for being born? We need make no apologies for being who we are. Nobody on planet earth is more or less valuable than you. Sometimes we need to be reminded of that, especially when our sense of self-worth is less than it ought to be.

Several years ago, an older friend of mine developed Alzheimer's disease. Bill had lived an active and productive professional life. But in his latter years, his wife cared for him at home. He was

119

aware of his increasing dependency on her and of the debilitating effect of the disease on his mind. Bill gave up everything he had ever done for himself until eventually nothing was left. As his mind suffered, his sense of worthiness also took a beating. He felt as if he were nobody.

There was one group to which he belonged that decided to stay with him during his decline. He sat on the University of Denver Board of Trustees and was encouraged by them to continue attending meetings as long as he was able. One of the board members drove Bill to the meetings and brought him back home afterward. This continued even after he had lost his ability to remember names, track a conversation or participate in any meaningful way.

His wife knew that he remained a board member in name only and that their decision to include him was made solely out of compassion. But Bill seemed to enjoy himself at the meetings and she reasoned that they were probably good for him. After he returned from one such meeting of the trustees, his wife asked him, "Did you have a good meeting, Bill?"

He thought for a moment before replying. Then he answered quite honestly, "I don't know." After a pause, he added this heartfelt comment: "But they still think I'm a people."

To them, he was somebody. To them, he mattered. He was still a person of value and worth.

He could no longer read or write or do any of the things that had been important earlier. But he was still "a people."

You need make no apologies for being who you are. You are a person of value – unique and beautiful. You are "a people" – unrepeatable and of infinite worth. That is something to celebrate!

The Way To Be Happy

A few years ago, a six-year-old boy from Oregon suffered burns over 85% of his body. His condition was so severe that several doctors gave up and one hospital would not admit him because they thought he would die anyway.

His life was saved, however, by eight courageous and committed people – his parents, three nurses and three doctors. The nurses emerged as the true heroines in this real-life drama. After other nurses had quit, these women took eight-hour shifts with the boy, seeing him through skin grafts, operations, crucial periods in which death almost gained victory, and dull, dragging days of rehabilitation. The boy grew to dislike them, as he innocently thought they caused his intense pain.

His room was like a dungeon. It measured 12 feet by 12 feet. The door was tightly shut, shades were drawn, heat blazed from a gooseneck lamp shining as a substitute for blankets. The humidity was so high the walls dripped with moisture, and

122

dank air smelled of burned flesh and chlorine-soaked dressings.

The nurses stayed with him, dressed in caps, gowns, masks and gloves as if they were assisting an operation. Within an hour they would be soaked with perspiration. For 14 desperately long months these dedicated three gave their all to the ailing boy. Then, one day, he finally climbed from his bed and walked.

It was a great day! The nurses were rewarded for their tireless effort. The lives of all three were so deepened and their sense of satisfaction so great after fighting off the temptation to quit for 14 months, that each said they'd put forth the effort again.

What caused them to feel so satisfied with their work? One might say it was because they found a way to truly serve someone in need. And in so doing, they accomplished something significant. Like American educator Booker T. Washington said, "Those who are happiest are those who do the most for others."

Someone observed, "It's easy to make a buck...it's a lot tougher to make a difference." But it's the way to be happy.

P.S.

"Life is hard. Then you die. Then they throw dirt in your face. Then the worms eat you. Be grateful it happens in that order."
~ Solomon Short

Something You Can't Fake

Comedian Tommy Smothers once quipped' "The best thing about getting older is that you gain sincerity. Once you learn to fake that, there's nothing you can't do."

Of course, faking sincerity is a lot like boasting about humility! It rather misses the point!

To be sincere is to be real. To be genuine. To be honest. And even...to be vulnerable. No easy task! Furthermore, sincerity begins with something that cannot be faked – honesty with yourself.

The Wall Street Journal once printed a little piece titled "Sincerity." It goes like this:

I wish I were big enough honestly to admit
all my shortcomings;
brilliant enough to accept praise without it
making me arrogant;
tall enough to tower above deceit;
strong enough to welcome criticism;
compassionate enough to understand

125

human frailties;
wise enough to recognize my mistakes;
humble enough to appreciate greatness;
staunch enough to stand by my friends;
human enough to be thoughtful of my neighbor;
and righteous enough to be devoted to
the love of God.

I may never be that strong, that compassionate, that wise or that loyal. But I can be genuine. And somehow, I know that will be enough.

Smile!

I am told that the muscles of the face are capable of over 250,000 different combinations of expressions. And one of the most useful is a smile.

Fulton J. Sheen used to say, "A smile across the aisle of a bus in the morning could save a suicide later in the day." That statement is true. We all need the healing medicine "of the heart" that a smile, even from strangers, provides. And for some, that medicine can save lives.

English essayist Joseph Addison put it this way: "What sunshine is to flowers, smiles are to humanity." Don't say you can't make a difference! Don't ever say you have nothing to give! Each of us can give a smile, spontaneously and sincerely. Its value may not be at once recognized, but be assured that it will be felt.

Smiling is infectious, you catch it like the flu,
When someone smiled at me today, I
started smiling too.

I passed around the corner and
someone saw my grin,
When he smiled I realized I'd passed it on to him.
I thought about that smile, then I knew its worth,
A single smile, just like mine, could
travel 'round the earth.
So, if you feel a smile begin, don't
leave it undetected;
Let's start an epidemic quick, and get
the world infected!

Today you will find plenty of occasions to pass along a heartfelt smile. Remember...it's the second best thing you can do with your lips!

P.S.

"My second favorite household chore is ironing. My first is hitting my head on the top bunk bed until I faint. ~ Erma Bombeck

Write The Other Way!

Henry L. Mencken said it first: "For every complex problem, there is a solution that is simple, neat and wrong." Several 7-Eleven stores learned the truth of that statement. According to a *New York Times* article, a number of the convenience stores had a problem with teenagers hanging out in their parking lots at all hours of the day and night. Not that they didn't like kids. But the teens were noisy. Customers had to walk around them to get into the stores. And they left discarded wrappers, cigarette butts and paper cups on the grounds.

Managers tried various methods to solve the problem. They asked the young people to move elsewhere. They asked them to pick up their trash. They even spoke to the police, but nothing worked. Each solution was simple, neat and ineffective.

Finally, one manager came up with an unusual idea to dissuade the teenagers from loitering in front of the stores. He suggested that all the shops start piping easy-listening music into the parking

130

lots. Immediately, the young people stopped hanging around. (Maybe his tactic was ruthless, but it worked!)

Sometimes we need a good answer. Again and again we butt up against the same old problem, whether it is relational, professional or personal. It seems that whatever we try is not working.

Perhaps you need to approach your persistent problem with a new way of thinking. The Spanish poet Juan Ramón Jiménez said, "If they give you ruled paper, write the other way." Is it time to exercise more creativity in your pursuit for the "right" answer?

I believe that humanity's best ideas have not yet been thought of. And the best solution for your problem may likewise be waiting to be conceived. It just might happen when you turn the paper sideways and write the other way!

Real Freedom

Two women happened to be seated next to each other on a plane and struck up an earnest conversation about their respective hometowns.

"Where I'm from," one woman sniveled, "we place all our emphasis on breeding."

Her new companion, unimpressed, smiled. "We think that's a lot of fun, too – but we do find time for other pursuits."

Some people value breeding, or social standing, or education, or money largely for the purpose of elevating their stature. They want to please and impress. They believe that to be "well-bred, well-fed, well-read and well-wed" will ensure a lifetime of happiness and success (and a satisfying bit of deference from others).

These symbols have little meaning for other individuals. They neither desire nor seek a higher stature in the eyes of others. The only power that interests them is power from within. The only standards which have meaning for them are those they

132

set themselves. The only person they really want to please and impress is the one looking back from the mirror. These individuals are truly free.

Entertainer Bill Cosby wisely said, "I don't know the key to success, but the key to failure is trying to please everybody." Who decides what is important to you? Who sets your standards? Ultimately, whom will you decide to please?

Answer these questions well and you will not only know happiness, you will be free!

P.S.

Why is it that the person who knows something the least also knows it the loudest?

I Call It Hope

Time magazine once reported a story that concerns itself with a woman in rural Florida who was recuperating from a lengthy illness. She enjoyed sitting on her front porch in her wheelchair and, on this day, she was watching her son work under his automobile. He had raised it on blocks of wood and removed the wheels.

Suddenly there was a lurch and the car fell on top of the boy! She screamed for her husband who ran to assist, but he could not budge the car. He climbed into his own vehicle and sped off for help.

The mother could hear that her son's groans were growing fainter and she knew she must do something. But how? She hadn't walked in months. Nevertheless, she realized that her son was dying before her eyes and that she was the only one to help.

She raised herself shakily to her feet and walked unsteadily to the car. Bracing herself, she

135

lifted. The car raised a few inches, just enough to let the boy scramble free. Then she collapsed.

After a thorough examination, she was found only to have suffered strained muscles. But the incredulous doctor's words were most telling: "I will always wonder," he said, "how far she might have lifted that car if she had been well and strong!"

Call it a miracle or call it a reserve of strength activated by a tremendous surge of adrenalin – this mother found what she needed to face the crisis. And so it is with all of us. You have strength, given by your Creator, to overcome seemingly impossible challenges ahead. You may feel weak or unable to cope, but you have been designed with sufficient power to meet those obstacles which may appear insurmountable.

Call it what you will. I call it hope.

Your Symphony

A high-powered corporate executive came into a doctor's office for a checkup. He showed signs of overwork and stress. He was warned to slow down, to take up a hobby – perhaps painting – to relax. He readily agreed.

The next day the executive phoned and announced enthusiastically, "Doc, this painting is wonderful! I've already done ten."

We don't need to be corporate executives to suffer from too much negative stress. It's easy to feel overwhelmed. You may be wondering this very minute whether you have time to read this page!

E.B. White once reported in the humor magazine *The Joyful Noiseletter* that turtles live an exceptionally long life. Scientists, he cited, are searching their blood for some clues to their longevity. He speculated that perhaps the turtles' blood vessels stay in such nice shape because of the way they conduct their lives. They rarely miss an opportunity to swim and relax in the sun. No two turtles ever lunched together with the idea of promoting something. They do not go to meetings and conferences. No turtle ever phoned another turtle back. They never use phrases like "implementation," "hard core," or "in the last analysis."

Maybe we don't need to be a turtle to find solace. Nor do we need to change jobs and move to the country. Slowing down and learning to hear the music, instead of clatter, can soothe one's soul in the midst of a busy life.

William Henry Channing gives us an excellent model for whole and happy living, free from negative anxiety and unhealthy stress. We can hardly do better than this:

"To live content with small means; to seek elegance rather than luxury, and refinement rather than fashion; to be worthy, not respectable, and wealthy, not rich; to study hard, think quietly, talk gently, act frankly; to listen to stars and birds, to babes and sages, with open heart; to bear all cheerfully, do all bravely, await occasions, hurry never. In a word, to let the spiritual, unbidden and unconscious, grow up through the common. This is to be my symphony."

P.S.

"Every year I live I am more convinced that the waste of life lies in the love we have not given, the powers we have not used, the selfish prudence that will risk nothing, and which shirking pain, misses happiness as well. No one ever yet was the poorer in the long run for having once in a lifetime 'let out all the length of the reins.'" ~ *Mary Cholomondeley*

Destined or Determined?

A sky-diving instructor was asked, "How many successful jumps must a student make before he or she can become certified?"

He answered, "All of them!"

Sky diving, however, is the exception. Is your life built on a series of successes? Do you usually attempt something new and immediately succeed, then succeed again and again? More likely, you may find that it is the other way around. Your successes are often built on smaller failures. You fell off the bike a few times before you learned to ride. And you produced a few culinary failures before you baked a successful layered cake or prepared a satisfactory omelet.

Tom Hopkins observes, "The number of times I succeed is in direct proportion to the number of times I can fail and keep on trying." And Winston Churchill stated, "Success is going from failure to failure without a loss of enthusiasm." They both agree that discouragement, rather than failure, is the enemy of success. Those who can remain hopeful and focused, though they fail, are those who will eventually succeed.

In all, Emily Dickinson is said to have written more than nine hundred poems. Though only four were published in her lifetime and the first volume of her poetry was not published until four years after her death, Dickinson's success is attributed to the fact that she did not allow discouragement to keep her from her poetry.

Where would we be today had Emily Dickinson lost her enthusiasm for writing? Because she kept her desire alive, we now remember her as one of the great poets of all time.

It's good to remember that success may be just beyond the next failure, and you'll get there, not because you're destined to, but because you're determined to.

Trouble's Gift

Mark Twain once said, "By trying, we can easily learn to endure adversity. Another man's, I mean." Actually, enduring other people's adversity is not always easy...especially when our loved ones suffer. But a vital ingredient to successful living is found in creatively handling our *own* problems.

We all face troubles. Daily. Some are no more than minor irritants; others will threaten our very lives. We can curse our problems. We can feel victimized by them. We can give in to them. We can also fight them. We can learn to live with them. And we can even use them – use them to help us do and become that which may have been impossible without them.

Case in point is Marvella Bayh, former wife of Indiana Senator Birch Bayh. She lost an eight-year struggle with cancer. It began with a mastectomy in 1971 and ended in 1979 when Marvella was 46 years old. But listen to the legacy of hope that she left millions of people:

"These years since cancer came to me have been the most rewarding, the most filling, the happiest in my life." Rewarding? Filling? Happiest? Is she really describing life with cancer? She goes on to say this:

"I have learned to value life, to cherish it, to put my priorities in order and to begin my long-postponed dream of being useful in my own right."

Since her mastectomy, Marcella Bayh devoted countless hours to American Cancer Society projects, supporting anti-cigarette crusades and promoting school programs to teach girls to examine their breasts for signs of cancer. One month before her death, she was awarded the society's Hubert H. Humphrey Inspiration Award.

Marvella Bayh's disease actually helped her to find fulfillment during the last years of her life. What many people never discover is that, when given a chance, problems can do that. Not that we should go out and try to find as much trouble as possible; as you know, trouble has a way of finding us. But those troubles, too, can be useful.

Writer Richard Bach says, "Every problem has a gift for you in its hands." Will you open that gift and discover just what it is that your adversity is giving you? For that very gift, which can only be obtained by going through those difficult times, may turn out to be valuable beyond belief.

P.S.

"When you come to the edge of all the light you know and are about to drop off into the darkness of the unknown, faith is knowing that one of two things will happen: there will be something solid to stand on or you will be taught how to fly." ~ Barbara Winter

Expect Something To Happen

Mildred "Babe" Didrikson was one of the world's greatest all-around athletes. Shep Steneman, in *Superhuman Achievements* (Random House, 1981), reports that she led her basketball team to a national championship in 1931. She set world records at the 1932 Olympics in the javelin throw and the 80-meter hurdles. And she went on to win every important women's golf tournament, including an amazing 17 in a row in 1946 and 1947.

But her greatest single performance was at the 1932 national track-and-field championships in Evanston, Illinois. Babe competed as a one-woman "team" against the best teams of female athletes in the country. She entered eight events and won five of them. She gave world-record performances in the baseball throw, javelin, and 80-meter hurdles, and matched a previous record in the high jump.

When the team scores were tallied up that day, the runner-up team of 22 women had a total of 22 points. Babe Didrikson alone had 30.

145

Few people will ever excel in a field as did Babe Didrikson. We can admire her, but few of us will ever *be* like her. Chances are, we may never be the very *best* at any one thing we set out to do. But being the "best" is not always what matters.

I like what a young boy said to a famous baseball player. Rabbi Wayne Dosick tells that he heard a youngster cheering on all-star outfielder Dave Winfield. "I expected the young boy to yell, 'Hit a homer, Dave,' or at the very least, 'Get a hit, Dave.' But instead this young man – well trained in the art of the possible – called out, 'Do your best, Dave. Do your best.'"

There are people who are silently calling to you: "Do your best. Do your best." Listen well. For those who play the best may win games, but winners in life are those who *do their best*, regardless of whether they *are the best*. They will eventually find joy and peace and an abundance of satisfaction.

One of life's greatest winners, Helen Keller, put it like this: "When we do the best that we can, we never know what miracle is wrought in our life, or in the life of another."

Do your best...and expect something good to happen!

All Used Up

A well-known surgeon was attending a dinner party and watched the host adroitly carve and slice the large turkey for his guests.

When he finished slicing, the host asked, "How did I do, Doc? I think I'd make a pretty good surgeon, don't you?"

"Perhaps," said the physician. "But anyone can take them apart. Now let's see you put it back together again."

Like surgery, some tasks require special talent, skill or training. Not everyone can be a surgeon. Many do not have the aptitude to teach a class or repair an automobile, nor can most of us cook a gourmet meal, play the piano expertly, or solve a complex mathematical problem. But we can each contribute.

Spanish cellist Pablo Casals said, "Don't be vain because you happen to have talent. You are not responsible for that; it was not of your doing. What you do with your talent is what matters."

147

On the other hand, don't be discouraged because you believe you have no ability. Each of us has much to offer. What you do with the ability you have is what matters.

Erma Bombeck was known for her humorous journalism. But she frequently seasoned her humor with pinches of wisdom. At the end of a newspaper column on March 10, 1987, Erma wrote these words:

"I always had a dream that when I am asked to give an accounting of my life to a higher court, it will go like this: 'So, empty your pockets. What have you got left of your life? Any dreams that were unfulfilled? Any unused talent that we gave you when you were born that you still have left? Any unsaid compliments or bits of love that you haven't spread around?

"And I will answer, 'I've nothing to return. I spent everything you gave me. I'm as naked as the day I was born.'" She would agree that what we do with the talent we're given is all that matters.

Do you still have some encouragement that you haven't spread around? Do you have ability you have not used up? Do you still have some bits of love to share?

If you were asked to empty your pockets today, will you find them half-full? Or will you discover that you have joyously spent everything you were given?

P.S.

"Dream as if you'll live forever. Live as if you'll die today." ~ James Dean

The "Good Old Days"

Does life seem to be more complicated than before? Too many plastic cards and *PIN* numbers and technology? One woman quipped, "I'd like to bank by phone, but I can't figure out how to get the money in those little holes."

Computers, of course, are supposed to make work more efficient. I love them – but I feel overwhelmed by their complexity at times. And I wonder how we became so dependent on them. Like when retired Rear Admiral Heintz Loeffler received a personalized computer-generated letter from a respected charity. It began, "Dear Rear...."

But I'd hate to go back to the B.C. era (before computers). With all its drawbacks and perplexities, progress has still carried us forward. After all, the "good old days" were never really that good.

Consider medicine. Early medical treatments too often relied on scientifically unproven potions and procedures. According to Dr. Herbert Benson in his audiotape *Timeless Healing* (Simon

150

& Schuster; 1996), so-called modern medicine in days of yore often did more harm than good. Patients endured purging, vomiting, poisoning, cutting, blistering, bleeding, freezing, heating, sweating, bleaching and shocking, and were advised to consume lizard blood, crocodile dung, pig's feet, worms and spiders. Almost all human and animal excretions were consumed or applied in medical treatments. Is that why the expression, "If it tastes bad, it's got to be good for you" became a cultural maxim?

We have come a long way and I don't want to go back. Better days are here today, and tomorrow can be the best yet. I believe that the rest of my life will be the best of my life. Let technology advance. But let me take care of the other areas of my life, too. I want to be a better person – starting from the inside. I want to constantly grow – to cultivate healthier attitudes, develop my character, accept greater responsibility for myself, make better decisions, sharpen my mind, care for my body, learn to love freely and nurture my spirit.

Do you believe that the rest of your life will be the best of your life? Will you help to make it so?

The Price Of Freedom

Have you ever been tempted to cut a corner or to take the easiest route, though you know it may not necessarily be the best one? Or have you ever made a decision because it was quick and simple, knowing that it might come back to bite you later?

I appreciate a parable Danish philosopher Soren Kierkegaard told about the dangers of taking the easy route. It is a story about a wild duck. Though life was difficult at times, the beautiful creature loved the boundless heavens and the endless stretches of wilderness. Soaring about treetops and towns, the duck symbolized, to its tame counterparts who could not fly, the epitome of freedom.

One evening during fall migration, he chanced to light in a barnyard where a farmer was feeding his ducks. The beautiful creature ate the corn the farmer sprinkled about and liked it so much that he stayed the night in a bed of warm straw. He ate the duck's corn again the next day. And the next. And the next....

When spring came, he heard his old companions flying overhead and an almost forgotten yearning awoke deep within. The duck had all but squelched his instinct for freedom over the comfortable and easy winter. But now he yearned to join his comrades in the sky. He flapped his stretched wings as he strained toward the flock, but he had grown fat and indolent and unable to fly. The wild duck had become a tame duck.

The easy way through our problems, though appealing, may not be the best way. It's always easier to borrow than to save; easier to jump in now than to do the hard work of planning; easier to postpone confronting a situation than to remedy it; easier to cut corners than to do it right; easier to remain the same than to make changes.

If you want to fly, you may have to pay a price. But freedom is worth it – at any cost!

Are you ready to soar?

P.S.

One student hung this sign around the neck of a skeleton in the school's anatomy lab: Waiting For The Perfect Man."

Need A Lift?

Father Kevin Sullivan, while serving a church in Decatur, Illinois, called the congregation's children to come forward for a special children's liturgy. Surrounded by one hundred of the church's youngsters, Fr. Sullivan said this to the parents: "I'm thankful for two things. I'm thankful for all these wonderful children with us here today. I love them all. And I'm also thankful for the gift of celibacy."

There is *always* something to be thankful for, and those who will look for reasons to give thanks will tap into one of life's most powerful emotions. For a thankful attitude can lift a life – spiritually, mentally and even physically – like nothing else.

One woman was asked why her hospitalized husband, who had been noticeably discouraged the day before, now seemed so much better. She explained that he had begun to improve day before when she had been sitting by his bedside, casually

155

touching a pearl necklace that he had given her years before. As she caressed the jewelry, a thought came to her.

"Mac," she said, "let's start thinking of every wonderful experience we've had in our lives, one for each of these pearls."

They started way back when they were first in love and that was the first pearl. Then they went along to their wedding day and then to their first baby. They continued recalling jobs, friends and everything else for which they were grateful, all the way down the string of pearls. "When we finished with the last pearl," she said, "all the dark shadows had gone and happiness reigned in our minds and in our hearts." This, she said, was the turning point in her husband's recovery.

The late Dr. Norman Vincent Peale, who first told this story (*In God We Trust;* Thomas Nelson Publishers, 1994), said, "You, too, can shift from gloominess to happiness, from dullness to vibrancy, from boredom to excitement. Wake up, change your thinking, and see how good life can be!"

Do you need a lift? Take some time to simply recall, one by one, all the good times in your life. Let yourself smile – and laugh! – and feel the pleasure you felt then. Make a list of these memories and keep it in a notebook so you can add to it often.

156

You may do this exercise alone or share it with somebody, but the more often you do it, the more pleasurable memories will come to mind. And the stronger those memories will become. It's simple. It's powerful. It's effective. And it just may be the lift you need.

No Time To Hurry

Igor Stravinsky was a disciplined composer who adhered to a rigid work schedule, carefully laid out in advance. Every minute of the day was taken up by some specific task.

On one occasion, his publisher asked him to hurry the completion of a new work. "I'm sorry," the composer said. "I haven't time in my schedule to hurry."

Our time is valuable. Many people feel that their time is more valuable than their money. And many people realize that they simply do not have time to hurry. They know what is important and they want what precious little time they have to count.

Dr. Howard Hendricks, a family counselor, learned the importance of taking enough time. One evening he asked his grown son what were some of his fondest childhood memories. His son replied, "Dad, it was the night you fixed my bike."

158

Dr. Hendricks could not even remember the evening, so his son recalled it for him. Hendricks was a university professor at the time. His evenings were often filled with meetings, and one evening in particular, he was rushing home to change clothes for an after-dinner speech he was to give at the school. As he drove up the driveway, he saw his son sitting on the ground beside his bicycle, anxiously waiting for Dad to come home. The handlebars were crooked and the front wheel needed alignment.

For some strange and wonderful reason, the professor asked his wife to call the school and say he would be late. Then he spent the next half-hour working with his son on the bike. And though he had forgotten the incident, years later his son still fondly recalled when his father took the time – to spend some time – as one of the best evenings of his life.

Time is precious. Do you really have time to hurry?

P.S.

"One touch is worth ten thousand words."
~ Harold Bloomfield

Touching Moments

I read that an insurance company survey revealed that spouses who kiss their mates in the morning will probably live five years longer than those who don't. It also showed that the kissing mate will have fewer auto accidents and up to 50% less time lost from work due to illness. I won't begin to interpret what all this means, except that it seems that those people in intimate relationships seem to be happier and healthier.

But what about that "touching moment" – that kiss? Is touch also important?

I once was asked to give some emotional support to a prisoner who was awaiting trial. We visited for a while in a prison conference room, talking about nothing more important than how long he may be incarcerated and whether or not he was guilty of the crime with which he was charged. He shared nothing of his deepest fears and yearnings. I felt as if we had not "connected" in any meaningful way.

161

Before I left, I took his hands. He held on tightly and dropped his head. No words were spoken – we just held onto each other. After a moment, he began to cry. As he sobbed, he held tightly to my hands. Somehow, the touch melted a dam of ice and now all his emotions gushed forth.

When his sobbing subsided, he began to talk once more. Only this time he spoke of his fear and loneliness and he told me of his concern for his family while he was imprisoned. All the while, he never let go of my hands, and I hung onto his. Because of the touch, he felt safe enough to share deeply.

People are crying out to be touched in caring and appropriate ways. (I know a woman who goes to a massage therapist once a week, even when she feels fine, just because she needs that dose of physical contact.) The lack of touch is one of the greatest impediments to emotional intimacy and happiness.

When film star Marilyn Monroe was asked if she ever felt loved by any of the foster families with whom she lived, she replied, "Once, when I was about seven or eight. The woman I was living with was putting on makeup, and I was watching her. She was in a happy mood, so she reached over and patted my cheeks with her rouge puff... For that moment, I felt loved by her."

Maybe you are in need of more closeness. And perhaps you know of those who are hungry for

162

some assurance that they are indeed loved; they are not alone. Your touch may accomplish what your words cannot – for those touching moments can change a life.

Index

Index, cont.

Quick Order Form

☞ Fax Orders: 413-431-3499. Send this form.

☞ Telephone Orders: Toll free: 877-344-0989

☞ Web Site Orders: visit
http://www.LifeSupportSystem.com/books

☞ Postal Orders: Life Support System Publishing P.O.
Box 237 Divide, CO 80814 USA

Order these books by Steve Goodier: $12.95
Colorado residents add sales tax: $.39 per book

❑ *One Minute Can Change a Life*   Quantity____
❑ *Riches of the Heart*   Quantity____
❑ *Joy Along the Way*   Quantity____
❑ *Prescription for Peace*   Quantity____
❑ *Touching Moments*   Quantity____

Name _____

Address:_____

_____

E-mail address_____

FREE Shipping and Handling for U.S.A. & Canada
Mexico: $2.00 / book. Other International: $4.00 / book

Would you like FREE gift wrapping?_____

Payment: ___ Check ___ Credit Card:
___Visa ___Master Card ___AMEX

Card #: _____Exp. date: _____

Receive daily inspirational e-mail FREE... visit:
www.LifeSupportSystem.com